D1270387

POLICE DEFUNDING AND REFORM:
What Changes Are Needed?

Olivia Ghafoerkhan and Hal Marcovitz

ReferencePoint
Press

San Diego, CA

About the Authors

Olivia Ghafoerkhan is a nonfiction writer who lives in northern Virginia. She is the author of several nonfiction books for teens and young readers. She also teaches college composition.

Hal Marcovitz is a former newspaper reporter and columnist who has written more than two hundred books for young readers. He makes his home in Chalfont, Pennsylvania.

For more information, contact:
ReferencePoint Press, Inc.
PO Box 27779
San Diego, CA 92198
www.ReferencePointPress.com

Picture Credits:
Cover: ChameleonsEye/Shutterstock.com
 6: Justin Berken/Shutterstock.com
10: Leonard Zhukovsky/Shutterstock.com
14: Associated Press
17: Imagespace/ZUMA Press/Newscom
23: Associated Press
28: katz/Shutterstock.com
33: Vic Hinterlang/Shutterstock.com
37: Maury Aaseng
41: Associated Press
47: Tippman98x/Shutterstock.com
51: Stan Godlewski/ZUMA Press/Newscom

LIBRARY OF CONGRESS CATALOGING-IN-PUBLICATION DATA

Names: Ghafoerkhan, Olivia, 1982- author. Marcovitz, Hal, author.
Title: Police defunding and reform : what changes are needed? / by Olivia Ghafoerkhan and Hal Marcovitz
Description: San Diego, CA : ReferencePoint Press, 2021. | Series: Being Black in America | Includes bibliographical references and index.
Identifiers: LCCN 2020048103 (print) | LCCN 2020048104 (ebook) | ISBN 9781678200268 (library binding) | ISBN 9781678200275 (ebook)
Subjects: LCSH: Police administration--United States--Juvenile literature. | Police brutality--United States--Juvenile literature. | Discrimination in law enforcement--United States--Juvenile literature. | Discrimination in criminal justice administration--United States--Juvenile literature. | Police--United States--Finance--Juvenile literature. | Racism--United States--Juvenile literature.
Classification: LCC HV8141 .G495 2021 (print) | LCC HV8141 (ebook) | DDC 363.2068--dc23
LC record available at https://lccn.loc.gov/2020048103
LC ebook record available at https://lccn.loc.gov/2020048104

CONTENTS

The Call to Defund the Police

George Floyd, a Black man, lost his life on a street in Minneapolis, Minnesota, on May 25, 2020, as a White city police officer pinned his knee into Floyd's neck. The officer, Derek Chauvin, and three other city police officers were attempting to arrest Floyd, who had allegedly used a counterfeit twenty-dollar bill to buy a package of cigarettes at a nearby convenience store.

In pinning Floyd to the ground during his arrest, Chauvin knelt on Floyd's neck for nearly nine minutes while Floyd begged for his life and said repeatedly that he could not breathe. Cell phone video of the tragedy was recorded by a witness, who uploaded the video to social media. The video quickly went viral, sparking global outrage. As in other instances of police killing people of color, protests erupted throughout America and in other countries. Activists called for police reform, but this time there also came calls to "defund the police," a phrase that has stirred controversy for its seemingly insistent plea to strip police departments of the support that ensures law enforcement in America.

The Minneapolis City Council promised dramatic changes in how police do their jobs. Among the proposals endorsed by several council members was one to disband the existing Minneapolis Police Department and rebuild the force. The rebuilt department would incorporate many progressive strategies, including largely eliminating the use of force by police officers. Said council president Lisa Bender, "It's our commitment to end policing as we know it, and re-create systems of public safety that actually keep us safe. It is clear that our existing system of policing and public safety isn't working for so many of our neighbors."[1] Mayor Jacob Frey responded by cutting police funding by $14 million in the city's 2021 budget.

> "It is clear that our existing system of policing and public safety isn't working for so many of our neighbors."[1]
>
> —Lisa Bender, Minneapolis City Council president

A few months after the pledge to rebuild the Minneapolis Police Department, crime rates climbed in the city, and citizens were left wondering if the council had made the right choice. Some council members walked back their support for the measure, claiming they endorsed the "spirit" of the decision but not the actual disbanding of the police force. With no replacement plan in place and council members showing some regret for their words, by late 2020 the fate of defunding and rebuilding the police in Minneapolis remained uncertain.

What Defunding Might Mean

Measures calling to defund the police are not new to police reform, though the phrase has become more popular as a rallying cry in light of the police killings in Minneapolis and other cities. To those who support defunding, the phrase implies a revisualizing of how policing is done. Some measures aim at shifting funds from police budgets to public and community services like housing, education, and mental health. These plans aim to deter crime by giving people a sense of purpose and commitment to their communities. The hope is that by helping residents better their lives, those trapped by poverty and a lack of social services would not turn to crime and end up in violent encounters with police.

Currently, police in America respond to a wide range of public ills that go far beyond violent crimes. Most of those who call

Outraged by the 2020 police killing of George Floyd, protesters took to the streets in Minneapolis (pictured) and other cities. Some protest signs displayed Floyd's last desperate words, while others demanded meaningful changes in policing.

for defunding the police imagine a world where more appropriate services would be called in to handle nonviolent situations. Counselors and social workers would address the needs of the mentally ill and drug abusers, for example. Police would then be limited to dealing with criminal activity, in which their expertise in crime solving and responding to potentially dangerous encounters is necessary.

The Objective Is Reform

Opponents of defunding argue that the aim is too radical. Over the years many city governments have found themselves short of funds, and rather than raise taxes—always a politically unpopular move—political leaders often order cutbacks in city services, including the police. As a result, police departments have often seen layoffs as well as budget cuts that have forced them to forgo equipment upgrades. Police supporters say officers are already asked to work long hours and put their lives in danger and that reduced funding just makes them more vulnerable. But defunding, they believe, sounds like ending financial backing for police entirely, leaving city streets barren of law enforcement.

Calls to defund the police remain part of the national conversation on police reform. While some believe reform is inevitable, they worry that terms like *defund* are too polarizing to bring about change, even if the events that sparked the calls are tragic. Says former New York City police commander James McCabe, "I am a proponent of good government and efficiency and not overspending on something that you shouldn't. But it might be a little bit of a knee-jerk reaction right now to just unilaterally defund the police because you don't like something that happened."[2]

As American cities continue to weigh the benefits and risks of reform policies, defunding the police has emerged as the cry of a public that will not tolerate the deaths of more people of color at the hands of police officers. Whether the push to defund the police will persuade communities and officials to adopt more radical ways of addressing the problem remains to be seen. Clearly, though, everyone involved in the conversation—from government officials, police reform activists, members of the public, and police officers themselves—hopes that whatever policies are put in place lead to a safer nation and more equitable law enforcement.

CHAPTER ONE

The Use of Force

Eric Garner was well known to the police in the New York City borough of Staten Island. A Black man, he had been arrested more than thirty times over the years, mostly for minor crimes such as marijuana possession and driving without a license. On many past occasions, Garner had been arrested for selling loose cigarettes on Staten Island streets—in other words, selling individual cigarettes that he had taken out of the packs he bought at neighborhood convenience stores. That is a crime in New York and other states.

On July 17, 2014, Garner was approached by several police officers as he allegedly sold loose cigarettes on the street. The officers told Garner he was under arrest. Garner denied selling the cigarettes. "Every time you see me, you want to mess with me," Garner told the police. "I'm tired of it. It stops today. I'm minding my business please just leave me alone."[3]

Garner tried to push his way past the police officers. A scuffle ensued as the officers attempted to restrain Garner, who stood 6 feet 3 inches (190.5 cm) tall and weighed 395 pounds (179 kg). During the scuffle one of the police officers, Daniel Pantaleo, placed his arms around Garner's neck and wrestled him to the sidewalk. As Pantaleo held his arms around Garner's neck, Garner muttered "I can't breathe" eleven times. When Pantaleo finally released his grip, Garner was unresponsive. An ambulance crew was summoned. When the emergency medical technicians arrived, they could not revive Garner. He was taken to a nearby hospital, where he was pronounced dead, a victim of suffocation.

Calls for Reform

The death of Garner is one of several cases that have prompted a movement in America to reform how police officers respond to incidents and employ force to arrest individuals—particularly Black individuals. On August 9, 2014, just three weeks after the death of Garner, Michael Brown was fatally shot by police on a street in Ferguson, Missouri. As in Garner's case, police suspected Brown, a Black man, was the perpetrator of a minor crime—shoplifting a package of cigars in a Ferguson convenience store. When police approached Brown, he attempted to flee. A scuffle ensued, ending when Ferguson police officer Darren Wilson fired twelve shots at Brown, six of which struck their mark.

The death of George Floyd six years later is regarded as yet another case in which police used excessive force against a Black citizen. Among the other notable cases is the 2020 death of Breonna Taylor, a Black woman who was asleep in her Louisville, Kentucky, apartment when police forced their way through the door under the mistaken belief the apartment was the headquarters of a drug trafficker. When Taylor's boyfriend fired his gun at the police, believing they were intruders, the officers riddled the apartment with bullets, killing Taylor.

These cases and others have prompted many people—including civil rights leaders, members of the public, and some elected officials—to call for reforms that would rein in the often violent and deadly methods police employ to subdue suspects. And while many activists have called for the elimination of the chokehold—the controversial arrest tactic employed by Pantaleo as well as Derek Chauvin in the Floyd case—they are in agreement that reforms must go further than simply banning neck restraints. "Banning neck restraints does not address the structural problems in the police department and does not address the cultural problem that we have about devaluing black folks," says Mike Griffin, a Black activist in Minneapolis. "We will be in this same exact moment in three months, in six months, in a year from now unless we change the significant structural problems of . . . the police department."[4]

9

A mural in Brooklyn, New York, depicts Eric Garner's death at the hands of police. Police use of force, especially in situations involving Black Americans, is one of the issues behind calls for police defunding and reform.

Following the deaths of Floyd and Taylor, many big-city mayors and members of city councils acknowledged that the police departments under their authority are in need of reforms. They have joined others in calling for significant changes in how police officers respond and make arrests. Says Lori Lightfoot, the mayor of Chicago, Illinois, "It goes without saying that the mayors in this country are accountable for what happens in our cities. And we feel a deep responsibility to the communities we serve. In fact, we owe them to make sure public safety is not just a feeling, but a reality."[5]

De-escalation Instead of Force

One way in which activists and political leaders hope to eliminate violent confrontations between police and citizens is through what is known as de-escalation. This is the idea that police would use nonconfrontational methods to ease tempers and avoid physical altercations when responding to a call that involves unstable individuals, hostility, or the potential for violence. Typically, when police are called to a scene where an individual is acting unruly, officers respond by attempting to restrain and arrest the person. This is the type of incident that often escalates into violent confrontation. The individual fights back, a scuffle ensues, and police often find themselves resorting to violent methods to subdue the suspect.

Advocates for de-escalation suggest that when police arrive at the scene, instead of literally pouncing on the individual, they would do well to pause and ask simply, 'What's wrong?' "Don't ask questions that can be answered yes or no, because I will guarantee you, you will get a yes or a no," says Paul Monteen, the retired police chief of Crookston, Minnesota, and an advocate for de-escalation training. "You won't find anything out. You need to open-end those questions. You know, 'What's bothering you? You're mad. How come you're mad?' — so that people will tell you what they're thinking about."[6]

> "You need to open-end those questions. You know, 'What's bothering you? You're mad. How come you're mad?'"[6]
>
> —Paul Monteen, retired police chief of Crookston, Minnesota

Studies have shown that de-escalation can be an effective method for resolving unruly situations before they turn violent. A 2016 study conducted by Campaign Zero, a group advocating for police reform, looked at arrest statistics for ninety-one police departments in the United States and concluded that police departments that employ de-escalation strategies are 38 percent less likely to resort to deadly force in making arrests. The study notes:

> We found that the . . . use of force policy restrictions adopted by police departments is a significant and influential factor in predicting the number of people killed by those departments. These results suggest that advocacy efforts focused on pushing police departments to adopt more restrictive use of force policies can produce meaningful reductions in the number of police-involved killings.[7]

Policing by Consent

In nineteen nations—among them the United Kingdom, Finland, Iceland, and Norway—deadly encounters with police rarely occur. The reason: Except under extraordinary circumstances, police in those nations do not carry guns. The police culture in those countries is based on the concept of policing by consent. In other words, law enforcement officials believe police should not exert their authority by instilling fear but rather gain authority by maintaining the respect and approval of the public.

Norway has been successful with this model of policing because its officers are highly trained in all aspects of policing, including de-escalation techniques. Also, police academies in Norway are very selective, accepting only 14 percent of the candidates who apply to them. Therefore, Norwegian police departments look for candidates who are naturally good at keeping their cool and as a result are unlikely to resort to using force. "The greatest skill a police officer can have is 'critical reflection,'" says Evar Oddsson, professor of sociology at the University of Akureyri in Iceland, which also does not arm police. "We need people who are cognizant of the fact that being a police officer is like being a social worker."

Quoted in Mélissa Godin, "What the US Can Learn from Countries Where Cops Don't Carry Guns," *Time*, June 19, 2020. https://time.com.

But critics argue that de-escalation does not always work. For example, if an individual is suffering from mental illness, they argue, that individual is not likely to respond to a dialogue intended to calm his or her emotions. Moreover, Chuck Wexler, executive director of the nonprofit Police Executive Research Forum, an organization focused on improving policing, points out that guns are so common in America that police must always be wary when they approach criminal suspects. Therefore, he says, police believe they will be less likely to provoke a gunfight if they move early to restrain the individuals. "That's why American police tend to be more cautious and protective," he says. "If somebody appears to have a bulge in their jacket, police get very nervous. You can't do anything with any of this unless the officer feels safe."[8]

Techniques Employed by Police

As Wexler suggests, many police officers are likely to draw their guns because they fear the unruly or otherwise suspicious people they are approaching may be armed. Virtually every police officer in America is armed and receives training in how to use a gun. And there are unquestionably good reasons for arming police officers. In what is known as an active shooter incident, police respond to calls in which a perpetrator, often armed with a semiautomatic weapon, is spraying a public area with gunfire. Police may be called to respond to armed robberies in progress—in which the perpetrators have their guns drawn and are threatening civilians in banks, convenience stores, and similar locations.

To deal with such situations, police officers need to be armed. Moreover, many big cities employ so-called special weapons and tactics (SWAT) teams. Members of SWAT teams are heavily armed, typically with rapid-firing weapons, and are often called in to active shooter situations and similar incidents in which violent confrontations are likely to erupt. Some city police departments have even procured military-style armored vehicles that are capable of crashing through walls. In essence, it can be concluded that most American police departments have the firepower they need to subdue armed and dangerous suspects their officers may encounter.

However, police officers are also trained in arrest techniques that do not require them to draw their weapons. Such techniques include the application of pressure to areas of the body that would cause distress to the individual, as well as takedowns—wrestling maneuvers intended to incapacitate the suspects. In Columbus, Indiana, for example, police academy students undergo three days of so-called physical tactics as part of their training. "Basically, it is Jiu-Jitsu, also known as ground fighting, for cops," says

13

Dave Steinkoenig, who teaches classes in physical tactics at the Columbus Police Academy. "A lot of the (training) is low impact. . . . There are very limited strikes, if you will. A lot of it is control techniques and leverage and, basically, if done properly, hopefully because you have that leverage, your opponent wears out long before you do and eventually gives up. That's the end goal."[9]

Chokehold Eliminated

Although police academy students are routinely taught many physical tactics, by 2020 the chokehold—otherwise known as the neck restraint—is one physical tactic that many American police departments had banned. The tactic, which was employed by Pantaleo to restrain Garner in 2014 and by Chauvin to restrain Floyd in 2020, has long been seen as a dangerous maneuver that frequently ends in the death of the suspect. Certainly, that was the outcome of the chokeholds employed in the arrests of Garner and Floyd.

Starting in the 1980s, use of the neck restraint was studied by a number of physicians, who concluded that police officers

Instructors demonstrate takedown and restraint techniques taught to law enforcement officers in Washington State. Techniques like these are meant to incapacitate suspects, not kill them.

should use the maneuver only when they believe their own lives are in danger. Wrote physicians Donald T. Reay and John W. Eisele in a 1982 study, "Neck holds must be considered potentially lethal under any circumstance and used only when there is no other alternative."[10]

Many police departments acted on those studies by banning the use of neck restraints. Among those police departments banning the chokehold, according to a 2016 study by the public policy group Reason Foundation, were Los Angeles, California; Philadelphia, Pennsylvania; and Seattle, Washington. But the study found that many police departments continued to permit the use of the technique. According to the study, among the cities that permitted the chokehold were New York City, where two years before the study was published, Garner died in a police-administered neck restraint; and Minneapolis, where Chauvin employed the chokehold against Floyd in 2020. And clearly, as cell phone video of the arrests of Garner and Floyd both illustrated, neither Pantaleo nor Chauvin were themselves in any physical danger when they acted to cut off the breathing passages of the men they were taking into custody.

> "If done properly, hopefully because you have that leverage, your opponent wears out long before you do and eventually gives up. That's the end goal."[9]
>
> —Dave Steinkoenig, instructor in physical tactics at the Columbus, Indiana, Police Academy

Police Reform Measures

The witness who recorded the cell phone video of Floyd's death uploaded the video to social media, where it was viewed by millions of people, prompting widespread demonstrations against police violence in Minneapolis and, within a few days, many other cities as well. Political leaders responded to those demonstrations and quickly enacted bans on neck restraints in their cities. In New York State, for example, the state assembly passed the Eric Garner Anti-Chokehold Act, banning the use of the neck restraint by police. (The New York City Police Department had actually banned its officers from using the chokehold in 1993, but court interpretations of the maneuver enabled police officers to continue to apply pressure to the neck—as long as they did not cut off the suspect's air supply.)

Chokeholds were not the only tactic banned as demonstrators took to the streets following Floyd's death in 2020. In the Breonna Taylor case, police burst into her apartment under the powers of a no-knock warrant, which gave them permission to enter the home without first announcing themselves. The confusion that erupted when police burst through the door led to police firing their guns, killing Taylor. (In all cases a search warrant must first be approved by a judge. In Taylor's case the police officers provided evidence to the judge that drug trafficking was taking place in the apartment, although this later turned out to be untrue. The judge responded by approving the no-knock warrant.)

Following Taylor's death, many city and state governments banned no-knock warrants, meaning that police must first announce why they wish to enter the home. For example, in June 2020, three months after Taylor's death, the Louisville Metro Council adopted Breonna's Law, banning the use of no-knock warrants in the city. Said Louisville mayor Greg Fischer, "I plan to sign Breonna's Law as soon as it hits my desk. I . . . wholeheartedly agree with Council that the risk to residents and officers with this kind of search outweigh any benefit."[11]

> **"I plan to sign Breonna's Law as soon as it hits my desk."[11]**
>
> —Greg Fischer, mayor of Louisville, Kentucky

Removing Qualified Immunity

While the bans on chokeholds and no-knock warrants were widely supported by many Americans, other plans to initiate police reform were met with a large measure of opposition. One proposal, which circulated in the US Congress following Floyd's death, was to remove the protection extended to police officers known as qualified immunity. Under state and federal law, quali-

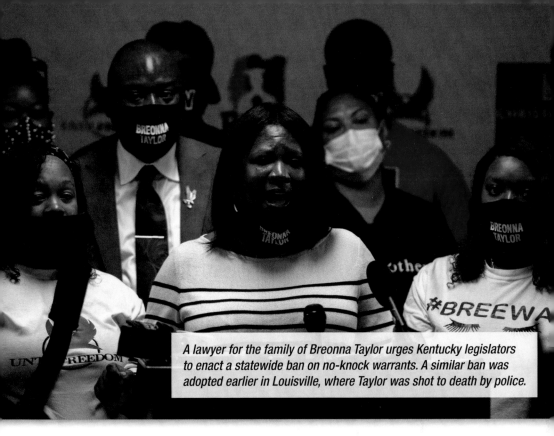

A lawyer for the family of Breonna Taylor urges Kentucky legislators to enact a statewide ban on no-knock warrants. A similar ban was adopted earlier in Louisville, where Taylor was shot to death by police.

fied immunity provides police officers with protections from civil lawsuits filed against them by the victims of police violence. In other words, without qualified immunity a police officer who fatally shoots a suspect in the course of an arrest could be found liable for monetary damages should a court rule the shooting was unjustified. Without the protection of qualified immunity, reformers argue, many police officers would be less likely to use excessive force while making arrests.

In fact, a June 2020 police reform bill written by Senator Tim Scott of South Carolina—the US Senate's lone Black Republican member—originally included a provision to peel back qualified immunity protection for police officers. But the bill was opposed by Larry Cosme, president of the Federal Law Enforcement Officers Association. The Washington, DC–based group is the chief lobbying arm for some twenty-six thousand law enforcement officers employed by sixty-five different federal agencies, among them the Federal Bureau of Investigation

The Fates of Daniel Pantaleo and Derek Chauvin

After Eric Garner died from the neck restraint applied by Daniel Pantaleo during his 2014 arrest, Pantaleo kept his job with the New York City Police Department but was ultimately fired in 2019. Following Garner's death, an investigative body known as a grand jury looked at the case and decided that Pantaleo committed no crime in detaining Garner with a chokehold. However, a five-year investigation by the police department's internal affairs unit concluded that Pantaleo had broken department rules by administering the chokehold. The police department banned neck restraints in 1993, but subsequent court interpretations of the ban found them to be permitted as long as the officer did not cut off the suspect's ability to breathe. The department's investigation concluded Pantaleo had violated the court's interpretation of a legal neck restraint.

Derek Chauvin, who administered the chokehold on George Floyd, is facing much more severe consequences. Chauvin was fired from the Minneapolis Police Department shortly after Floyd's death. He was charged with second-degree murder and faces up to forty years in prison if convicted at a trial expected to occur in 2021. He was able to post $1 million in bail in October 2020, enabling him to return home to await trial.

(FBI) and US Immigration and Customs Enforcement. Lobbyists use their influence to support or kill legislation that affects their members.

Cosme read Scott's bill before it was introduced in the Senate and immediately saw that its provisions included stripping federal law enforcement officers—as well as members of city and state police departments—of qualified immunity. He quickly used his influence to win a meeting with US attorney general William Barr. After he told Barr that his organization opposed the bill's proposal to remove qualified immunity, Barr agreed to press Scott to strip the language out of the bill. "Attorney General Barr assured us it wouldn't go that far,"[12] Cosme said. A few days later, Scott introduced the bill in the Senate. By then, the provision stripping police officers of qualified immunity had been removed from the proposed legislation. Scott's legislation did not win enough votes to move out of the Senate. Democratic members opposed the legislation, claiming it was too weak and did not go far enough to institute true police reforms.

Nevertheless, the deaths of Garner, Floyd, Taylor, Brown, and many other victims of police violence have prompted political leaders to make changes. Neck restraints are now widely banned in American police departments. No-knock warrants have been banned by numerous states and cities. Many police departments are now mandating that their academies provide or emphasize de-escalation training to students. These changes show that in recent years, many American political leaders have recognized that the use of force has become too imbedded in the culture of their police departments, and they are prepared to take the necessary steps to change that culture.

CHAPTER TWO

The Call for Transparency and Accountability

Derek Chauvin, the Minneapolis police officer charged with employing a lethal chokehold on George Floyd, had been a member of his city's police department since 2001. During his career on the Minneapolis police force, Chauvin had been accused of misconduct at least seventeen times prior to the night of May 25, 2020, when Floyd lost his life. Among those seventeen cases, only two resulted in disciplinary action. In each case, Chauvin received a letter of reprimand from his superiors.

This information about Chauvin was revealed in the weeks following the death of Floyd. The Minneapolis police did not willingly release the information. Rather, it was unearthed by members of the media as they dug into Chauvin's background. After press reports revealed Chauvin's record of misconduct, the Minneapolis police acknowledged that there had been cases of wrongdoing filed against Chauvin but refused to provide details on exactly what Chauvin did to merit the letters of reprimand—or even why it found no cause to consider misconduct charges against Chauvin in the other fifteen cases.

The fact that Chauvin's past record of misconduct was kept secret is troubling to advocates for police reform, who believe the public has a right to know whether the men and women charged with enforcing the law have themselves been accused of breaking the law. "[Confidentiality] makes it really tough for the public to know just who it is they are dealing with and to know whether their department or any particular officer is one they would want out in the streets,"[13] says David Harris, a University of Pittsburgh law professor who studies police behavior.

> "If you don't think you're going to get caught, who cares if you're recorded? Who cares if someone's looking?"[14]
>
> —Olugbenga Ajilore, an expert on police misconduct for the Center for American Progress

Moreover, reform advocates suggest that the culture of secrecy found in many police departments illustrates how the departments themselves might be guilty of covering up the crimes of their members. They point to the fact that Chauvin was well aware that nearby witnesses were using their cell phones to record his abuse of Floyd. Olugbenga Ajilore, an expert on police misconduct for the Washington, DC–based public policy research organization Center for American Progress, says:

> That officer knew he was being videotaped, still killed the guy, and knew there was nothing that would happen. Think about it, if you go to a store and try to steal something and someone has a camera on you, you're going to stop right? You're afraid you're going to get caught. But if you don't think you're going to get caught, who cares if you're recorded? Who cares if someone's looking?[14]

Misconduct Shielded from the Public

Advocates for police reform argue that if new degrees of transparency and accountability are brought to the culture of law enforcement, incidents of police misconduct could be greatly reduced. In other words, if the public is given access to information about police misconduct and if the outcomes of investigations into misconduct are made public, police officers would be on notice that everything they do would be subject to the highest degrees of public scrutiny.

Over the years, accusations of misconduct against police officers have been largely kept secret due to laws enacted by various states. A 2017 study by WNYC, the public radio broadcaster in New York City, determined that twenty-three state governments prohibited access by members of the public to records of police misconduct.

Moreover, the fact that nearly half of state governments have barred access to records of police misconduct also illustrates the power wielded by the labor unions that represent police officers. For many years, union leaders have pressured state legislators to enact laws that bar public access to records of police misconduct.

When it comes to labor relations, police officers are no different from many other American workers. They are represented by labor unions that negotiate salaries, vacation time, health care, and other benefits. But unions representing police officers have gone much further, demanding that police departments bar public access to the disciplinary actions initiated against their members.

Police union leaders argue that misconduct records should be kept private because of the nature of police work. In making arrests, police officers often have to confront dangerous or mentally unstable individuals, who might later wish to seek revenge for their arrests. The unions argue that opening up private police personnel records to members of the public could help those vengeful individuals locate the homes of police officers and endanger them and their families. "The unfettered release of police personnel records will allow unstable people to target police officers and our families for harassment or worse," says Patrick Lynch, head of the Patrolmen's Benevolent Association,

> "The unfettered release of police personnel records will allow unstable people to target police officers and our families for harassment or worse."[15]
>
> —Patrick Lynch, head of the Patrolmen's Benevolent Association of New York City

the union that represents New York City police officers. "A danger-ous cop-hater only needs a police officer's name, linked to a few false or frivolous complaints, to be inspired to commit violence."[15]

Calls for a National Database of Police Misconduct

While police union leaders have been very effective in keeping misconduct records out of the purview of the public, advocates for police reform have faced another significant hurdle. Currently, there is no effective way to manage the tremendous volume of in-formation that would suddenly be opened to access should mem-bers of the public be granted permission to view the records. By 2020 there were nearly seven hundred thousand police officers employed by more than eighteen thousand police departments in the United States. Wading through those records would present a formidable task.

Over the years, efforts have been made to create a police mis-conduct database, although those efforts have not focused on mak-ing individual cases accessible to public scrutiny. Rather, the goal has been to identify use of force and misconduct trends among

A sketch artist depicts a court hearing in which former Minneapolis police officer Derek Chauvin (right) appears on closed-circuit television from prison. Records uncovered by the media revealed a history of misconduct complaints filed against Chauvin.

individual departments and states. In 1994 Congress passed a law enabling the FBI to collect data chronicling incidents in which police employed the use of force against suspects, but the law lacked provisions to compel police departments to provide the information.

Nor did the law provide funding to help departments compile the data—an obvious gap for many of the tiny police departments that patrol rural communities. Matthew Hickman, a criminal justice professor at Seattle University in Washington State, says:

> They made it a federal law but Congress did not appropriate any funds to actually do the job. It's not like you flip a switch and data flows in from 18,000 agencies—it's challenging. . . . This kind of thing will tend to hit smaller agencies the hardest, where in some cases, all personnel—including the chief—are out on patrol and have little spare time to comply with federal data collections.[16]

In 2015 Congress updated the law, empowering the FBI to create the National Use-of-Force Data Collection project. After receiving the mandate to create the database, then-director of the FBI James Comey said, "It's ridiculous that I can't tell you how many people were shot by the police in this country last week, last year, the last decade—it's ridiculous."[17]

Again, though, participation in the FBI's data collection project has been voluntary. Since the project was created in 2015, only about 40 percent of police departments in the United States have provided data to the FBI. Geoffrey Alpert, a criminology professor at the University of South Carolina, suggests that the police departments reporting the data are likely to be departments that see few cases of misconduct in their ranks. He says, "The only agencies willing to report this were those feeling good about their data."[18]

Police Officers Charged with Crimes

In the wake of the massive protests following Floyd's death—and the revelation of the many misconduct claims against Chauvin—

The Case of One Rogue Police Officer

One consequence of ensuring that police misconduct is kept out of the public record is that if a police officer is fired from his or her job due to misconduct, the officer often has the freedom to find employment on another police force. Reform advocates point to the case of Sean Sullivan to illustrate how the system often ensures that rogue police officers are not held accountable for their misconduct.

In 2004 Sullivan was fired from the Coquille, Oregon, police department after he was caught kissing a ten-year-old girl on the lips. He was also criminally charged in the case, and as part of his sentence was barred from seeking employment elsewhere as a police officer. But officials in the small town of Cedar Vale, Kansas, had no access to Sullivan's prior employment records. Three months after he left Coquille, Sullivan was hired not as a police officer in Cedar Vale, but as the town's police chief.

Eventually, Sullivan lost that job as well after he was investigated for sexual assault and burglary. By 2020 Sullivan was imprisoned in Washington State on charges of possessing the illegal drug methamphetamine.

members of Congress proposed measures to mandate that police departments provide information to the data collection project. Congress also considered legislation enabling the federal government to provide financial assistance so individual departments could carry out the congressional mandate. But again, the police unions stepped in to thwart the measures.

For example, the original June 2020 police reform bill written by Senator Tim Scott of South Carolina included language to create a national database of police misconduct. But like the provision to peel back qualified immunity protections for police, that provision was taken out of the bill after Larry Cosme of the Federal Law Enforcement Officers Association pressured Attorney General William Barr to delete the language. Cosme says his association would continue to oppose creation of a national police misconduct database. "We're not going to abdicate our rights," says Cosme. "We're going to come out swinging. We're not going to back down."[19]

While efforts to create a national police misconduct database stalled in 2020, independent efforts to gather data on misconduct have shown that many police officers have, in fact, broken the law. In 2019 five California newspapers collaborated on an effort to track down cases of police misconduct in the state. Reporters unearthed evidence that 630 California police officers were criminally charged between 2008 and 2018.

Typical offenses committed by the officers included drunken driving and domestic violence. One officer charged in a drunken driving case was the acting police chief in Riverside, who wrecked his police cruiser when he crashed into a wall. In another case, a deputy sheriff in Santa Clara County was found to have been responsible for the deaths of two bicyclists after he dozed off at the wheel, crashing his car into the victims.

The efforts by the California journalists illustrate that some police officers do break the law, but without a national police misconduct database the public is largely unaware of these cases. "Given the power that police have—if you have cops with those kinds of records, it's sort of a betrayal of the public trust,"[20] says Roger Goldman, a law professor at Saint Louis University in Missouri.

> "Given the power that police have—if you have cops with those kinds of records, it's sort of a betrayal of the public trust."[20]
>
> —Roger Goldman, law professor at Saint Louis University in Missouri

State Legislatures Change Their Laws

The cases unearthed by the journalists in California as well as the revelation that Chauvin had a long history of misconduct charges filed against him has prompted some state legislatures to make misconduct records available. In fact, a few months prior to the investigation conducted by the newspapers, California governor Jerry Brown signed the state's Peace Officers: Release of Records Act, which requires police departments to make public

Derek Chauvin's Misconduct

During his nineteen-year career with the Minneapolis Police Department, Derek Chauvin was charged at least seventeen times with misconduct, twice receiving letters of reprimand from his superiors. But details of those seventeen cases have largely been kept out of the public record by the Minneapolis police—even after Chauvin was charged with the murder of George Floyd.

Following Chauvin's arrest, though, several individuals stepped forward to report the specifics of the complaints they leveled against the officer. In May 2020 Kristofer Bergh told a BuzzFeed reporter that he was seventeen years old in 2013 when he and his friends were approached by Chauvin and another Minneapolis police officer after one of the young people allegedly fired a Nerf gun that may have struck a passerby. A Nerf gun is a toy that shoots harmless foam pellets. According to Bergh, Chauvin approached the teens with his gun drawn.

Bergh said he filed a complaint against Chauvin, insisting there was no reason for the officer to draw a weapon on the teens. Minneapolis police later emailed him an apology which stated, "I apologize that you had a negative interaction with our Officers." According to the news organization BuzzFeed, Chauvin was not disciplined in this case.

Quoted in Tasneem Nashrulla, "Minneapolis Officer Derek Chauvin Had 17 Complaints Against Him Before He Was Charged with Murder for George Floyd's Death," BuzzFeed News, May 29, 2020. www.buzzfeednews.com.

misconduct reports in which officers are accused of excessive force, sexual assault, and other crimes. The bill that Brown signed into law was authored by Nancy Skinner, a state senator from the California community of Berkeley. She says, "For law enforcement to do their job, they need the community's trust. When you block access to information from the public, that trust will not be there. . . . If you have a record, it's disclosable."[21]

The New York State Assembly also took action to make police misconduct records available to the public. In June 2020 the assembly repealed a law enacted in 1976 that shielded such records from public review. The assembly's action brought to a

close a long campaign by Constance Malcolm to convince legislators to repeal the law. In 2012 Malcolm's eighteen-year-old son Ramarley Graham, who was Black, was fatally shot by White New York City police officer Richard Haste. The officer followed Graham to his house from a nearby store, forcing his way into the teen's home. Haste told a grand jury investigation that he believed Graham was armed, but in fact, Graham was unarmed. The grand jury elected not to criminally charge Haste.

Malcolm spent the next eight years trying to gain access to Haste's personnel records to find out whether he had been accused of other acts of misconduct, but she was barred due to the 1976 law. When New York governor Andrew Cuomo signed the repeal of the 1976 law, Malcolm said, "Now families like mine and people who are brutalized by police won't have to rely on leaks to get information about the officers who abused them. So this is a very big victory for us."[22]

Establishing Citizen Review Boards

While police reform advocates have made strides in forcing police departments to be more transparent, they also acknowledge that they still have a long way to go to ensure that the officers are held accountable for their deeds. In the case of the California newspaper investigation, for example, the journalists found that of the 630 police officers who were charged with crimes in the previous decade, 80 of those officers were permitted to keep their jobs. Indeed, how police departments investigate conduct by their own officers is often not disclosed. Also, the standards the departments maintain—deciding what level of misconduct merits suspension or dismissal and what levels merit a letter of reprimand—are also rarely disclosed by police officials.

For example, in the Santa Clara County case, deputy sheriff James Council was able to keep his job despite the fact that the two bicyclists, Kristy Gough, age thirty, and Matt Peterson, age twenty-nine, were killed when they were struck by his car. "Was justice served? Absolutely not," says Jon Orban, a friend of the victims. "When someone holds a badge they should be held to a higher standard; in this case he wasn't held to any standard at all. I don't know of an organization where if you kill two people you get to keep your job."[23]

One way in which advocates hope to make police officers more accountable for their misconduct is to take the review of their cases out of the hands of their superiors and instead create civilian review boards to investigate and pass judgment on the cases. Some communities have already established such boards to oversee their police departments. A 2018 study coauthored by Olugbenga Ajilore found that some 150 American communities have appointed civilian boards to oversee the investigation of police misconduct cases. Ajilore and coauthor Shane Shirey write:

> Civilian oversight boards are not a catch-all solution to excessive police force, but they can help to hold police accountable and reduce instances of the unnecessary use

of force. Effective oversight boards also hold the promise of enhancing public safety and renewing public trust in police, especially within African American communities. But not all boards work equally well. To succeed, civilian oversight boards need resources and authority to maintain accurate data, and foster robust relationships with city officials and community members. Above all, they must operate independently of police departments themselves.[24]

But even efforts to establish civilian review boards have been met with opposition by police labor unions. In 2016, for example, the city council of Newark, New Jersey, voted to establish a civilian review board to investigate police misconduct cases in the community. The move was immediately opposed by the Newark chapter of the Fraternal Order of Police, the union representing the city's officers. The union challenged the establishment of the civilian review board in court, and in 2020 the union received a favorable ruling from the New Jersey Supreme Court. The court denied the review board the power to subpoena witnesses—meaning the board held no power to compel police officers or others to testify before the panel. Says Newark mayor Ras Baraka, "At this time in our nation's history, where the world watched the barbarism of Officer Chauvin as he murdered George Floyd with a knee on his neck, the New Jersey Supreme Court's action is out of step with national sentiment, and failed to remove the knee off the necks of many of us in New Jersey."[25]

Many police unions and political leaders oppose greater transparency and accountability that would expose wrongdoing by police officers. Although some communities have taken steps toward transparency and accountability, such as establishing civilian review boards, the fact that only about 150 such boards are in existence illustrates that advocates for police reform still have many hurdles ahead as they try to hold rogue police officers accountable for their misconduct.

CHAPTER THREE

Demands to Defund the Police

The call received in April 2020 at the Austin, Texas, 911 dispatch center alerted authorities that a potentially deadly scene was unfolding in an apartment complex parking lot. The caller reported that a man and a woman were sitting in a car in the parking lot, using drugs. The caller also said the two occupants of the car were arguing and that the man had pointed a gun at the woman's head. "They're in the car smoking crack and cooking meth," the caller told the police dispatcher. "He has a gun to this lady. . . . I seen him holding a gun. . . . He's holding it up."[26]

The 911 dispatcher alerted police, and moments later eight Austin police officers arrived at the scene. They ordered the man in the car to leave the vehicle and raise his hands. The man in the car, Michael Ramos, a person of Black and Latino descent, complied with the officers' orders. He stepped out of the car and raised his hands. As he stood in the parking lot with his hands up, Ramos told the police officers, "I ain't got no . . . gun. Why all of y'all got guns?"[27]

A police officer ordered Ramos to step forward. He refused. At that point, one of the officers fired a so-called bean bag round at Ramos. The projectile is a bullet encased in a padded fabric cushion. When it strikes an individual, the bean bag round does not pierce the body. Rather, it is intended to cause a nonlethal dose of pain that is supposed to temporarily immobilize the individual, giving police the opportunity to take the suspect into custody. In this case, though, the bean bag round appeared to have no effect on Ramos. After he was struck in the thigh by the bean bag round, he turned, walked away from the police officers, reentered his car, and began backing out of the parking place.

Another officer, Christopher Taylor, responded by opening fire on the car. Ramos was struck by the gunfire and died at the scene. The whole incident was recorded on videos shot by body cameras worn by the police officers. Later, an investigation revealed that no gun was found in Ramos's car. Says Scott Hendler, an attorney retained by Ramos's family, "Nothing I saw in the videos has changed my opinion that the shooting was unjustified and that Michael Ramos was not a threat—to officers, to himself or anyone else."[28] As for Taylor, by the end of 2020 he remained employed by the Austin police but was on administrative leave, meaning he was not permitted to report for work. The case remained under investigation by authorities seeking to determine whether Taylor's shooting of Ramos was justified.

What Is Meant by "Defunding the Police"

The shooting of Ramos did not initially spark protests in the streets of Austin, but following George Floyd's death a month later, protesters did pour into the streets of the Texas city and call attention to the Ramos case. In Austin as well as other cities, many protesters shouted demands to "defund the police."

By demanding that city council members defund the Austin police, protesters were not calling for a total withdrawal of taxpayer dollars from the city police department—meaning that calls to defund the police would not leave the city without police protection. Rather, police reform advocates like those in Austin have asked for portions of budgets earmarked for police departments to instead be set aside for social programs. In their view, programs that help improve the lives of low-income people or people who are experiencing problems related to mental illness or addiction will reduce interactions with police. In other words, instead of outfitting a new SWAT team with the latest assault gear and rapid-firing weapons, that money would, for example, be spent on hiring mental health counselors. Mental health counselors, rather than police, would respond to emergency situations involving troubled individuals. This would be in addition to programs aimed at reducing illegal drug use, alcoholism, and violent acts—situations that often lead to interactions with police.

Carleigh Sailon, a clinical social worker in Denver, Colorado, says angry and erratic individuals react far differently when they are approached by mental health counselors than by armed police officers in uniform. "The uniform alone can be a trigger for people depending on what their past experience has been, especially if

Protesters and police face off in May 2020 in Austin, Texas. Protesters called attention to the police killings of George Floyd in Minneapolis and Michael Ramos in Austin and demanded the defunding of police.

they have a history in the criminal justice system," she says. "Even if the officer is being supportive, they can have an immediate fear that they're in trouble or going to jail."[29]

Fewer Police Often Means High Crime

The idea of defunding police, even partially, has many detractors. Opponents of defunding the police argue that cutting police budgets—and therefore the number of officers who patrol city streets—often leads to higher crime rates. Due to a budget shortfall, in 2011 the city of Newark, New Jersey, was forced to lay off 15 percent of its police officers. That year, Newark experienced a 65 percent increase in the city's homicide rate. Other violent crimes, such as shootings and assaults, rose 21 percent.

Also in 2011, Sacramento, California, faced a financial shortfall as well. To make up the budget gap without raising taxes on residents, Sacramento officials ordered cuts in the police department. Specifically, Sacramento made cuts in the city's narcotics squad as well as the units that investigate street gang violence, automobile thefts, and prostitution. Police were told not to respond to minor traffic accidents. Almost immediately, Sacramento saw its crime rate increase. Shootings rose by 48 percent over the previous year. The number of rapes, robberies, assaults, burglaries, and vehicle thefts also increased.

West Virginia attorney general Patrick Morrisey believes this outcome will be repeated as government officials cut police department budgets. He warns:

> Taking away funding for local, county, and state law enforcement will lead to an increase in crime, drug overdoses, violence, vigilantism, and inequality. It is definitely proper

"The uniform alone can be a trigger for people depending on what their past experience has been, especially if they have a history in the criminal justice system."[29]

—Carleigh Sailon, clinical social worker in Denver, Colorado to examine the need for reforms with police interaction—particularly in communities of color. However, gutting police departments is not the answer to a much deeper problem. Police officers save lives. Having more cops on the streets has been shown to reduce crime.[30]

Reimagining Public Safety in Austin

Nevertheless, in the wake of the Ramos shooting, Austin elected to move money out of its police department and into social services programs. For 2020 the Austin City Council appropriated

Al Sharpton Opposes Defunding the Police

Opponents of the movement to defund American police departments found an unexpected ally in the Reverend Al Sharpton, for decades one of the nation's most vocal Black civil rights leaders. During the summer of 2020, municipal leaders in many American cities slashed their police budgets and moved money into community-based programs to improve the quality of life in urban neighborhoods. But Sharpton called for cities to resist demands to defund and instead fully fund their police departments.

Sharpton says Black-on-Black crime remains a significant problem in cities, and police are needed to protect innocent Black citizens. "On the side of the city that I come from, which is Blacker and poorer, we've seen more in terms of gun usage," Sharpton says. "I got a lot of attention when I did the eulogy for George Floyd's funeral, but I also, a month later, preached a 1-year-old kid's funeral in Brooklyn [New York] who was killed by a stray bullet."

Sharpton says police departments need to be reformed so that officers are better able to respond to incidents without first drawing their guns. But police departments need to be adequately funded, he says. "People living on the ground need proper policing," Sharpton says.

Quoted in Brian Flood, "Al Sharpton: Defunding Police Is Something 'a Latte Liberal' May Like, but 'Proper Policing' Is Necessary," Fox News, September 8, 2020. www.foxnews.com.

$434 million to the city's police department. But for the 2021 budget, the council stripped $150 million out of the police budget. Instead, the council allocated money to a number of new services intended to provide alternative responses to situations that often lead to police drawing their guns. For example, council members put $50 million into a new program it named the Reimagine Safety Fund. The focus of this fund is to provide alternative responses to erratic or unruly behavior by individuals.

Instead of using the police to provide those services, grants from the Reimagine Safety Fund will be made available to community-based organizations that propose new ways to respond to emergency situations. City officials hope organizations will offer new plans for mental health and substance abuse counseling as well as programs to find affordable housing for the homeless.

These changes do not mean that Austin will be without a police force. While the city council cut funding to the police department, it still approved nearly $300 million to finance police operations. Some believe this is not enough for a functioning police department. Texas governor Greg Abbott was critical of the council's action, warning that officers and residents of Austin will find their safety compromised by these changes. Says Abbott, "Austin's decision puts the brave men and women of the Austin Police Department and their families at greater risk, and paves the way for lawlessness. Public safety is job one, and Austin has abandoned that duty."[31]

Crisis Response Teams

Austin was not the only American city to approve plans to defund its police department. For example, Los Angeles officials agreed to cut $150 million out of the city's $1.8 billion police budget and reallocate that amount toward social services programs (such as mental health counseling) in minority communities. Los Angeles officials also determined that a lot of the calls police officers respond to could probably be handled by city workers who do not show up with badges and guns. The Los Angeles City Council created a new unit that would dispatch crisis responders to nonviolent incidents in

How Americans View Police Defunding and Other Reform Proposals

A July 2020 poll by the Gallup organization reveals that many Americans (58 percent) believe that major changes in policing are needed, but not all reforms have equal support. And support varies even more when the results are broken down by race and ethnicity. In all categories, abolishing police departments has the least support. However, about half of all Americans (and significantly more Black Americans) favor ending officer involvement in nonviolent crimes and shifting money from police departments to social programs.

Americans' Support for Policing Reform Options, by Race/Ethnicity

	All Americans	Black Americans	Asian Americans	Hispanic Americans	White Americans
Changing management practices so officers with multiple incidents of abuse of power are not allowed to serve	98%	99%	98%	99%	97%
Requiring officers to have good relations with the community	97%	97%	98%	96%	97%
Changing management practices so officer abuses are punished	96%	98%	99%	96%	95%
Promoting community-based alternatives such as violence intervention	82%	94%	91%	83%	80%
Ending stop and frisk	74%	93%	89%	76%	70%
Eliminating police unions	56%	61%	68%	56%	55%
Eliminating officer enforcement of nonviolent crimes	50%	72%	72%	55%	44%
Reducing the budgets of police departments and shifting the money to social programs	47%	70%	80%	49%	41%
Abolishing police departments	15%	22%	27%	20%	12%

Source: Steve Crabtree, "Most Americans Say Policing Needs 'Major Changes,'" Gallup, July 22, 2020.

which mediation, not force, is used to quell tempers. "We need to reimagine public safety in the 21st century," says Los Angeles City Council member Herb Wesson Jr. "One which reduces the need for armed police presence, especially when the situation does not necessarily require it."[32]

In New York City, the city council cut the $6 billion police budget by $484 million. Among the cuts in the police budget was the hiring of only twelve hundred new police officers for 2021. (The New York City Police Department employs thirty-six thousand police officers.) That money will instead be spent on programs intended to guide young people away from criminal activities. In addition, New York

The Sunnyvale Model of Policing

The city of Sunnyvale, California, provides public safety to its citizens in a manner considered unique in America. The city of 140,000 residents near San Francisco does not have a police department but rather a department of public safety. Employees of the department serve as police officers as well as firefighters and emergency medical technicians.

The city has combined all three tasks into one department since 1950 and has found that its officers are not regarded as armed authoritative figures—as they are in many big-city police departments—but rather as respected public servants who can respond to burglaries, extinguish fires, or provide emergency medical care to accident victims. "Because firefighters are often seen by community members as caretakers, people will help you out," says Phan Ngo, chief of the Sunnyvale Department of Public Safety. "So, I do think to a certain extent, it does have a positive impact in what we do here in our city."

Ngo suggests that instead of defunding the police, cities would do well to look at the way Sunnyvale provides public safety. "I wish that this model could be implemented everywhere," he says. "I'm a firm advocate for this public safety model."

Quoted in Kai Ryssdal and Bennett Purser, "How One City Provides Public Safety Without a Police Department," Marketplace, June 10, 2020. www.marketplace.org.

intends to create a program in which members of the community are selected to act as liaisons who can represent their neighborhoods in disputes with police. These community ambassadors will be given access to police commanders under a plan to quickly bring complaints about police misconduct to senior members of the department. "These ambassadors will reflect the diversity of the [city] and serve as liaisons between officers and New Yorkers," says New York City mayor Bill de Blasio. "This new initiative will provide a venue to address complaints and concerns, and ensure [the New York City Police Department] leadership hears New Yorkers."[33]

Several other cities, among them Seattle, San Francisco, Baltimore, and Washington, DC, took similar steps. Most often they cut police budgets and redirected the money into social services programs or created teams of unarmed civilian mediators to take over some of the tasks formerly assigned to police. Members of those communities as well as many other cities endorsed those changes. A July 2020 survey by the national polling group Gallup reported that a majority of Americans support changing the way police departments respond to incidents. According to the poll, 58 percent of Americans said "policing needs major changes."[34] In addition, 47 percent of all Americans—including 70 percent of Black Americans—favor reducing police department budgets and shifting the money to social programs.

A significant number of participants—96 percent—said that changes are needed in the management of police departments to ensure that abusive officers are punished. Moreover, 82 percent of the respondents to the polls said more emphasis should be placed on community-based solutions to urban problems, such as more mental health counseling, substance abuse counseling, and family services counseling that would help steer young people away from criminal acts. "People realize they need the police [while] looking for the police to be more accountable and transparent," says Brenda Bond-Fortier, a professor of public policy at Suffolk University in Boston, Massachusetts. "We want to be thinking about where can kids interact with the police in situations outside of a 911 call— schools, maybe, playgrounds or community events."[35]

Making Reforms Without Defunding

Many cities elected not to cut their police budgets but still saw the need to find ways to deal with minor incidents that did not necessarily require the presence of police. In Chicago, Arturo Carrillo, an organizer for the mental health advocacy group Collaborative for Community Wellness argues that a person in need of mental health counseling often does not receive assistance until police show up, arrest that person, and incarcerate him or her in the city jail.

Once in jail, Carrillo says, the person's mental health is evaluated, and counselors are assigned to the inmate. He suggests that the inmate could have received treatment much quicker, and without the need for police involvement, if a crisis response professional showed up at the scene and used his or her training to evaluate the person and call in mental health counselors right away. "Currently, the city's response to crises has been done and managed exclusively by the city's police department," says Carrillo. "As a result, the largest mental health provider in this city is the . . . county jail."[36] Chicago officials elected not to cut the city's $1.2 billion police budget but remained open to Carrillo's proposal. In September 2020 a measure known as the Treatment for Trauma Bill that would create crisis management teams to respond to such incidents was introduced in the Chicago City Council.

By late 2020 the council had not yet acted on the proposal, but members of the city's governing body were supportive of the plan. Says Carlos Ramirez-Rosa, a member of the Chicago City Council, "We need a non-law enforcement emergency crisis response to ensure that when people are in need of help . . . they will get the support that they need, and it will not result in an unnecessary arrest, and it will not result in an unnecessary murder or death at the hands of law enforcement."[37]

The Death of Walter Wallace Jr.

No such team was in place in October 2020 when Philadelphia police were summoned to an urban neighborhood where an individual was storming through streets in obvious distress. When police arrived, they found Walter Wallace Jr., a twenty-seven-year-old Black man, wielding a knife. The police officers drew their guns and ordered Wallace to drop the knife. Wallace refused and instead charged the officers. Police responded by fatally shooting Wallace. Later, investigators determined that Wallace suffered from a mental illness known as bipolar disorder. People who suffer from this disorder typically experience episodes of depression—times in which they cannot motivate themselves even to rise from bed—as well as manic episodes, when they become easily agitated, exercise irrational behavior, possess enormous energy, and are unable to calm themselves. When Wallace charged the officers, he was likely trapped in the manic phase of his illness.

The fatal shooting of Wallace touched off several days of protests in the city, some of which turned violent as demonstrators clashed with police. For several days Governor Tom Wolf was forced to summon Pennsylvania National Guard troops to help keep order on city streets. Meanwhile, Philadelphia mayor James Kenney instituted a curfew that endured for nearly a week, banning people from the streets after 9:00 p.m. each night.

When protests over the police shooting of Walter Wallace Jr. turned violent in Philadelphia in October 2020, the governor summoned the Pennsylvania National Guard. Guard members (pictured) were there to help keep order on city streets.

Shaka Johnson, an attorney retained by Wallace's family, said that when Wallace's wife called 911 to report her husband's conduct, she specifically told the dispatcher that Wallace suffered from bipolar disorder and was acting irrationally. Johnson believes the police officers who responded were unprepared to confront an irrational person suffering from mental illness. "Officers who are properly trained should notice certain things when they arrive at a scene," Johnson says. "Especially when his wife tells you, 'Stand down officers, he's manic bipolar.'"[38]

> "Officers who are properly trained should notice certain things when they arrive at a scene. Especially when his wife tells you, 'Stand down officers, he's manic bipolar.'"[38]
>
> —Shaka Johnson, attorney retained by the family of police shooting victim Walter Wallace Jr.

Earlier in the year, in the wake of George Floyd's death, the Philadelphia City Council approved a modest police defunding plan, agreeing to move $33 million out of the $760 million city police budget. Although a $33 million cut sounds significant, in reality the city council made the cut by eliminating a $19 million budget hike requested by police and then moving police functions that cost $14 million into other city agencies. Those functions included the department that administers the crossing guards who halt traffic in front of schools so that students can safely cross streets, as well as the bureau that oversees public safety officers who write tickets for cars parked illegally on city streets. The public safety officers have no other police powers.

No part of the police defunding measures approved by the Philadelphia City Council went toward creating a force of crisis responders who may have reacted differently when confronted by a knife-wielding man and perhaps could have used their skills and training to talk him down from his manic episode. Kris Henderson, executive director of the Philadelphia-based Amistad Law Project, which advocates for civil rights, points out that had mental health counselors been dispatched to the scene rather than police, it is likely that Wallace would still be alive. Henderson says, "There's so many situations that the police show up and other people could do that job better."[39]

CHAPTER FOUR

How Cities Are Reforming Their Police Departments

For decades the city of Camden, New Jersey, bore a notorious reputation as a haven for drug dealers and other criminals. By 2012 nearly two hundred street corners in the city of seventy-five thousand people were used by pushers to sell drugs. Thefts, burglaries, armed robberies, and other crimes were rampant as well.

At the core of Camden's ills was its police department, which was plagued by corrupt police officers. Police were found to have been fabricating evidence against citizens, which enabled prosecutors to win convictions and resulted in jail sentences for innocent people. In 2012 city officials found themselves facing civil lawsuits brought against the police department by eighty-eight people who had been wrongfully convicted of crimes due to evidence that was fabricated by police. Eventually, the city government agreed to pay $3.5 million to those individuals to settle the cases.

City leaders in Camden knew they would have to take dramatic steps to reform their police department. And so in 2012 they completely dismantled the police department and then rebuilt the force. New leaders were brought in from outside. Every Camden police officer was fired and then invited to reapply for jobs in the new department. Ultimately, only about one hundred of the city's four hundred police officers were rehired for jobs in the new department. "Back then residents of Camden city absolutely feared the police department and members of the department. [The] residents wanted that to change,"[40] says Louis Cappelli, a Camden freeholder. (A freeholder is an elected official in New Jersey communities.)

Within a few years, residents of Camden came to know a much different police department. When new recruits are hired by the Camden police, they are required to knock on doors in the neighborhoods where they are assigned to introduce themselves to the residents. At the police academy, they are schooled in de-escalation techniques so that when they arrive at the scene of a disturbance, they can act as mediators and resolve heated situations without drawing their guns. Camden's citizens are predominantly Black and Latino; therefore, when recruiters seek new officers, they first look to hire Black and Latino applicants.

> "We want to make sure residents of the city know these streets are theirs."[41]
>
> —Louis Cappelli, Camden, New Jersey, freeholder

It is not unusual for police officers in Camden to host neighborhood picnics and barbecues. Police officers also organize movie nights on vacant lots, showing family-oriented films. On one evening in 2020, police officers hosted an outdoor screening of the animated film *The Lion King* on a neighborhood block that was formerly so infested with drug dealers that it was known locally as Heroin Highway. Says Cappelli, "We want to make sure residents of the city know these streets are theirs. They need to claim these streets as their own, not let drug dealers and criminals claim them."[41]

Eliminating Qualified Immunity

Camden rebuilt its police force eight years before George Floyd's death on a Minneapolis street—the incident that prompted the national protests demanding that cities reform their police departments. As mayors, city council members, and other elected officials saw thousands of protesters fill their

The CAHOOTS Program in Oregon

The CAHOOTS program in Eugene, Oregon, is an alternative to traditional policing. CAHOOTS—the initials stand for Crisis Assistance Helping Out on the Streets—is a collaboration between the local police and White Bird Clinic, a mental health service. When 911 dispatchers determine that callers are experiencing mental health issues, they route these calls to the CAHOOTS team. The team consists of a medical professional—either a nurse, paramedic, or emergency medical technician—as well as a social worker trained to respond to crisis situations. Says Ebony Morgan, a CAHOOTS crisis worker:

> I came into this work passionate about being part of an alternative to police response because my father died during a police encounter. So it matters to me very much. . . . I think policing may have a place within this system, but I also think that it's over-utilized as an immediate response because it just comes with a risk. And it's a risk that crisis response teams that are unarmed don't come with. You know, in 30 years, we've never had a serious injury or a death that our team was responsible for. . . . And I think that models like this can help people have support in their community and feel safer within their community.

Quoted in Ari Shapiro, "'CAHOOTS': How Social Workers and Police Share Responsibilities in Eugene, Oregon," National Public Radio, June 10, 2020. www.npr.org.

streets demanding change, many realized they would need to undertake large-scale change just as city leaders in Camden had eight years earlier.

One place where government officials acted quickly was Colorado. On June 13, 2020, the state legislature passed a new law titled the Enhance Law Enforcement Integrity Act, which eliminated the qualified immunity protection for law enforcement officers in the state. When Governor Jared Polis signed the legislation into law, Colorado became the first state to allow victims of police violence to bring lawsuits against officers. Under the new law, individuals can seek monetary damages of as much as $25,000 from officers who have physically abused them.

Rob Pride, a police sergeant in the Colorado community of Loveland, says he is concerned that the new law may force police officers to put themselves in harm's way. He suggests that police officers may be slow to use force in situations that may warrant such tactics as they consider whether too much force would expose them to lawsuits and ultimately make them personally responsible for injuries they cause. As police momentarily delay their responses as they mull over their options, he says, the individuals they are facing may draw their weapons and use them. "I'm worried for my guys," Pride says. "When we hesitate, there's a good chance that we don't go home at the end of the day."[42]

But Colorado state representative Leslie Herod, who authored the legislation, says police would do well to understand that the use of force should always be their last option. Says Herod, "If officers are rethinking [their careers] because of a law of integrity and accountability, then they shouldn't be in the profession as a police officer. Their duty is to serve and protect, not kill. It is very important that law-enforcement officers think before they act."[43]

> "I'm worried for my guys. When we hesitate, there's a good chance that we don't go home at the end of the day."[42]
>
> —Rob Pride, Loveland, Colorado, police sergeant

Also in Colorado, in June 2020 the city of Denver instituted a new response protocol for 911 calls that report individuals who are suffering from mental health and substance use episodes and are in need of emergency care. Instead of the call going first to nearby police officers, a mobile crisis intervention team is now dispatched to the scene. Members of the team include paramedics as well as physicians qualified to assess mental illnesses. The teams respond to 911 calls reporting attempted suicides as well as drug overdoses and similar situations that have in the past resulted in responses by police.

After the Camden, New Jersey, police department was dismantled, it was rebuilt to better reflect the racial and ethnic diversity of the community. Today's force (some of whom are shown at a 2019 award ceremony) is actively involved in the community.

Reforms in Minneapolis

Given that the national call for police reform grew out of an incident on a Minneapolis street that cost George Floyd his life, many civil rights leaders called attention to the city's police department and demanded change. And city officials did at first promise dramatic change, suggesting that the city should rebuild its police force much the same way Camden had eight years earlier. Indeed, in the days following the death of Floyd, several city council members signed a pledge to "end policing as we know it."[44] But political leaders in Minneapolis soon backed away from such dramatic change, insisting that they never intended to dismantle the police department and instead would seek reforms within the existing department. "I think the initial announcement created a certain level of confusion from residents at a time when the city really needed that stability," says Minneapolis mayor Jacob Frey, who did not support the pledge. "I also think that the declaration itself meant a lot of different things to a lot of different people—and that included a healthy share of activists that were anticipating abolition."[45]

The RIGHT Care Teams in Texas

In 2018 government leaders in Dallas, Texas, saw the need for a response to people suffering from mental health issues without calling on police to arrest them. That year, the first RIGHT Care team began working in the city. The team responds to 911 calls for people having mental health crises. A RIGHT Care team consists of a police officer, a paramedic, and a social worker.

Officials in Dallas initiated the program after several incidents in which police used force to subdue mentally ill individuals. The most prominent case occurred in 2013 when two Dallas police officers shot a man suffering from bipolar disorder when he stood on a chair and wielded a knife. The man did not approach police officers with the knife.

Since 2018, RIGHT Care teams have responded to more than six thousand calls. Says Dallas police officer Dontario Harris, a member of a RIGHT Care team, "Having a third party with us who specialized in social work kind of takes a lot off of our shoulders because we are not licensed or specialized in that area. So having that avenue is a big help to us and to the community. This is really changing the outlook on how people look at policing, which helps me."

Quoted in Hunter Davis, "Texas Program's New Response to Mental Health-Related 911 Calls Changing 'How People Look at Policing,'" Fox News, July 20, 2020. www.foxnews.com.

Instead, Minneapolis city leaders looked to the Minnesota Legislature to enact police reforms for the entire state. And in July 2020 state lawmakers enacted a bill that addresses several reform goals. For example, the bill bans chokeholds except in situations in which the officers believe their lives are in jeopardy. The new law also provides financial incentives for police officers to live in the cities they patrol. Following the death of Floyd, leaders of the Minneapolis police acknowledged that only 8 percent of the city's 873 police officers actually live in the city—the others are residents of nearby suburbs. Police reform advocates insist that police officers will feel much more empathy for the city's residents—and be far less likely to use excessive force against them—if they actually live in the communities they patrol. Leaders of the Black community believe that when White police officers live in urban neighborhoods, it can help defuse racial friction between White officers and Black citizens. "There's some white people that actually only know black people by what they've ever heard," says Keyon Jackson-Malone, a Black resident of Milwaukee, Wisconsin. "There's no experience. There's no, 'I went to school with 30 of them.'"[46]

Despite the reform measures adopted by the state government, many Black civil rights leaders in Minneapolis contend that the measures did not go far enough. They have criticized Minneapolis City Council members for backing away from their pledge to dismantle and rebuild the city police force. Miski Noor, an organizer with the Minneapolis civil rights group Black Visions Collective, complains that a majority of council members in the city are White and therefore out of touch with the needs of the Black community. "A majority-white . . . board of people can't decide that they knew better than the community," says Noor. Moreover, Noor predicts that since the city council did not approve widespread reform measures, police violence would continue in Minneapolis. "What kind of violence are we going to experience over the next year?"[47] she asks.

Police Unions Protest in Connecticut

While government officials in Minneapolis were criticized for backing away from true police reform, in Connecticut government leaders were criticized for going too far. In Connecticut, such criticisms were raised by leaders of police unions following adoption of a new law by state legislators that makes police misconduct records available for public scrutiny. Specifically, the law prohibits the state government as well as municipal governments from including language in police union contracts barring the public release of misconduct records.

Andrew Matthews, president of the Connecticut State Police Union, complains that the new law represents a knee-jerk reaction by the legislature to the death of Floyd—an incident that occurred more than 1,000 miles (1,609 km) from the Connecticut state border. "We think it was an emotional decision," Matthews says. "Continuously, in their argument, the state mentioned Mr. Floyd. Mr. Floyd was not murdered here in Connecticut. Our troopers do not conduct themselves in that way."[48] The Connecticut law also removes qualified immunity protection for police officers. "If this portion of the bill is passed, police officers would fail to act when necessary for fear of being sued," says Matthews. "Once you start telling officers that they're going to be potentially financially responsible for something they're doing for you, as the employer, I think that people will reconsider and go elsewhere to other professions, if they can leave."[49]

But advocates for police reform have defended the new measures. "We're tired of police trying to be the victim when they're abusing and killing people," says Barbara Fair, a civil rights activist in New Haven, Connecticut. "If an officer is doing his job, doing it correctly, then they will not have to worry about any liability."[50]

Implicit Bias Training in Texas

In Texas, officials initiated a far different strategy from the measures imposed in Connecticut, Colorado, and Minnesota. Rather than trying to change the way police officers do their jobs, Texas officials have focused on preparing officers to have different viewpoints of policing before they are assigned to their beats. Specifically, Texas officials are trying to eliminate what are known as implicit biases among police officers.

By embracing implicit bias training, government leaders are essentially saying that police officers need to recognize their own biases. Implicit biases are deep-rooted prejudices people may harbor toward members of an ethnic group, religious faith, nationality, or the gay or non-binary communities. People may harbor those prejudices due to incidents that have occurred in their lives, through talking with other people, through interpretations of what they may have seen in the news media, or through varieties of other sources. Unconsciously, they have drawn biased conclusions about members of specific groups.

When police officers harbor implicit biases, the people they are biased against may find themselves under suspicion. In such cases, for example, White police officers may regard innocent Black civilians as suspects in crimes.

Implicit bias training seeks to help people recognize their biases and understand that their biases are wrong and unfounded. In June 2020, at the request of Garnet Coleman, a Black state representative from Houston, the Texas Commission on Law

Disagreement over police defunding and reform measures is as strong in Connecticut as in other states. But in one Connecticut city, Hamden, police and activists marched side by side in June 2020 (pictured) in an effort to start an honest and open dialogue.

Enforcement—which sets training standards for Texas police academies—started requiring all police officers to undergo implicit bias training. "Implicit bias can distort one's perception and subsequent treatment, of a person or group," says Coleman. "Implicit bias training for law enforcement personnel is designed to help them identify and remove bias from their decision-making process and encourage more objective behavior. This training for law enforcement will help them better serve and protect the public."[51]

Officials in Texas took other steps as well to update training methods for police officers. For example, in addition to implicit bias training, the Texas Commission on Law Enforcement also added de-escalation techniques to the required training programs for police officers. Also, police officers in Texas are now given training in recognizing symptoms of mental illness among people they encounter on calls.

> "Implicit bias training for law enforcement personnel is designed to help them identify and remove bias from their decision-making process and encourage more objective behavior."[51]
>
> —Garnet Coleman, Texas state representative

Drawbacks to Defunding

As communities in Connecticut, Texas, Colorado, and Minnesota have implemented new measures to reform police departments, the controversy over such measures has continued. In the days following the death of Walter Wallace Jr. in Philadelphia, new calls to defund the police were shouted as demonstrators marched through the streets. Earlier in the year, in response to the death of Floyd, the city government had made the modest cut in the police budget amounting to $33 million, but following Wallace's death, police reform advocates and many elected officials demanded more. Advocates point out that in the Wallace case, the dispatcher was alerted that Wallace was mentally troubled.

In contrast, though, opponents of defunding argued that diverting money from the police department to mental health crisis teams and similar purposes would have its drawbacks. Wallace was shot as he approached the two Philadelphia police officers with a knife. Afterward, investigators concluded that the proper tactic for the officers would have been to stun Wallace with a Taser—a nonlethal device that emits an electric charge, used to momentarily incapacitate a person. However, in the Wallace case, neither officer was equipped with a Taser. In fact, two-thirds of Philadelphia police officers do not carry Tasers because the police department lacks the funds to purchase the devices. John Street, a former Philadelphia mayor, says, "This is a failure of leadership. We take nine months to train someone to be a member of the Philadelphia Police Department. We spend tens of thousands of dollars. It is inexcusable for those police officers to be there without the proper equipment. . . . That situation should have never have happened."[52]

Nevertheless, some members of the Philadelphia City Council say they intend to press on and introduce a plan to divert tens of millions of dollars from the city's police budget into programs that would provide nonpolice response teams, mental health care, drug and alcohol counseling, and more affordable housing opportunities for city residents. This debate illustrates the rethinking of how policing is performed in American society. In the wake of Floyd's death and other incidents of police misconduct, America is finding new ways to ensure the safety of the public as well as rethinking the powers granted to police departments responsible for maintaining law and order.

Introduction: The Call to Defund the Police

1. Quoted in Derek Hawkins et al., "'Defund the Police' Gains Traction as Cities Seek Solutions," *Washington Post*, June 8, 2020. www.washingtonpost.com.
2. Quoted in Simon Weichselbaum and Nicole Lewis, "Support for Defunding the Police Department Is Growing. Here's Why It's Not a Silver Bullet," Marshall Project, June 9, 2020. www.themarshallproject.org.

Chapter One: The Use of Force

3. Quoted in Noah Rayman, "New York Man Dies After Police Try to Arrest Him," *Time*, July 18, 2014. https://time.com.
4. Quoted in Alicia Victoria Lozano and Daniella Silva, "'Who Else Needs to Die?': Calls for Police Reform Intensify Amid George Floyd Protests," NBC News, June 11, 2020. www.nbcnews.com.
5. Quoted in Diane Pathieu and Mark Rivera, "Lightfoot's CPD Reform Strategy Includes 'Co-responder' Model, Replacing Officers in Some Situations," ABC 7, August 13, 2020. https://abc7chicago.com.
6. Quoted in Curtis Gilbert, "Not Trained to Not Kill," American Public Media Reports, May 5, 2017. www.apmreports.org.
7. Samuel Sinyangwe, "Examining the Role of Use of Force Policies in Ending Police Violence," Campaign Zero, September 20, 2016. https://static1.squarespace.com.
8. Quoted in Erin Schumaker, "Police Reformers Push for De-escalation Training, but the Jury Is Out on Its Effectiveness," ABC News, July 5, 2020. https://abcnews.go.com.
9. Quoted in Andy East, "Use of Force: Local Officers Explain How Defensive Tactics Are Taught, Monitored and Performed," *Columbus (IN) Republic*, June 13, 2020. www.therepublic.com.

10. Donald T. Reay and John W. Eisele, "Death from Law Enforcement Neck Holds," *American Journal of Forensic Medicine and Pathology*, September 1982, p. 257.
11. Quoted in Barbara Campbell, "No-Knock Warrants Banned in Louisville in Law Named for Breonna Taylor," National Public Radio, June 11, 2020. www.npr.org.
12. Quoted in Luke Broadwater and Catie Edmondson, "Police Groups Wield Strong Influence in Congress, Resisting the Strictest Reforms," *New York Times*, June 25, 2020. www.nytimes.com.

Chapter Two: The Call for Transparency and Accountability

13. Quoted in Associated Press, "Police Disciplinary Records Are Largely Kept Secret in US," WTTW, June 13, 2020. https://news.wttw.com.
14. Quoted in Haven Orecchio-Egresitz, "Derek Chauvin Had 16 Complaints Made Against Him That Were Closed with 'No Discipline.' A Former Member of the Police Review Board Says That's Proof of a Broken System," Insider, May 29, 2020. www.insider.com.
15. Quoted in Associated Press, "Police Disciplinary Records Are Largely Kept Secret in US."
16. Quoted in Vera Bergengruen, "'We Continue to Spin in Circles.' Inside the Decades-Long Effort to Create a National Police Use-of-Force Database," *Time*, June 20, 2020. http://time.com.
17. Quoted in Bergengruen, "'We Continue to Spin in Circles.'"
18. Quoted in Bergengruen, "'We Continue to Spin in Circles.'"
19. Quoted in Broadwater and Edmondson, "Police Groups Wield Strong Influence in Congress, Resisting the Strictest Reforms."
20. Quoted in Robert Lewis and David DeBolt, "California's Criminal Cops: Investigation Finds 630 Officers Convicted of Misdemeanors. Many Are Still Working," *Palm Springs (CA) Desert Sun*, November 10, 2019. www.desertsun.com.
21. Quoted in Marco della Cava, "When Police Misconduct Occurs, Records Often Stay Secret. One Mom's Fight to Change That," *USA Today*, October 14, 2019. www.usatoday.com.

22. Quoted in Stephanie Wykstra, "The Fight for Transparency in Police Misconduct, Explained," *Vox*, June 16, 2020. www .vox.com.

23. Quoted in Lewis and DeBolt, "California's Criminal Cops."

24. Olugbenga Ajilore and Shane Shirey, "How Civilian Review Boards Can Further Police Accountability and Improve Community Relations," Scholars Strategy Network, June 25, 2018. https://scholars.org.

25. Quoted in Ian T. Shearn, "State Supreme Court Limits Powers of Newark's Civilian Review Board," *New Jersey Spotlight*, August 20, 2020. www.njspotlight.com.

Chapter Three: Demands to Defund the Police

26. Quoted in Katie Hall, "Austin Police Release Video Footage of Michael Ramos Shooting," *Austin (TX) American-Statesman*, July 27, 2020. www.statesman.com.

27. Quoted in Hall, "Austin Police Release Video Footage of Michael Ramos Shooting."

28. Quoted in Hall, "Austin Police Release Video Footage of Michael Ramos Shooting."

29. Quoted in Lindsay Schnell, "Defund Police? Some Cities Have Already Started by Investing in Mental Health Instead," *USA Today*, June 22, 2020. www.usatoday.com.

30. Patrick Morrisey, "'Defund the Police' Movement Is Deeply Misguided," *Weirton (WV) Daily Times*, July 18, 2020. www .weirtondailytimes.com.

31. Quoted in Meena Venkataramanan, "Austin City Council Cuts Police Department Budget by One-Third, Mainly Through Reorganizing Some Duties out from Law Enforcement Oversight," *Texas Tribune*, August 13, 2020. www.texastribune.org.

32. Quoted in Saba Hamedy and Topher Gauk-Roger, "Los Angeles City Council Moves Forward with Plan to Replace Police Officers with Community-Based Responders for Nonviolent Calls," CNN, June 30, 2020. www.cnn.com.

33. Quoted in NYC.gov, "Mayor de Blasio Announces New Policing Reforms," June 7, 2020. www1.nyc.gov.

34. Steve Crabtree, "Most Americans Say Policing Needs 'Major Changes,'" Gallup, July 22, 2020. https://news.gallup.com.

35. Quoted in Ben Guarino, "Few Americans Want to Abolish Police, Gallup Survey Finds," *Washington Post*, July 20, 2020. www.washingtonpost.com.
36. Quoted in Michael Lee, "Crisis Response Team—Without Cops—Would Be Sent to Mental Health Emergencies Under Proposal," *Chicago Sun-Times*, September 29, 2020. https://chicago.suntimes.com.
37. Quoted in Lee, "Crisis Response Team—Without Cops—Would Be Sent to Mental Health Emergencies Under Proposal."
38. Quoted in Ellie Rushing et al., "Walter Wallace Jr., 27, a 'Family Man' with Many Mental Health Crises and Encounters with Police," *Philadelphia Inquirer*, October 27, 2020. www.inquirer.com.
39. Quoted in Oona Goodin-Smith and Anna Orso, "Renewed Calls to Defund the Police," *Philadelphia Inquirer*, November 2, 2020, p. A4.

Chapter Four: How Cities Are Reforming Their Police Departments

40. Quoted in Scottie Andrew, "This City Disbanded Its Police Department Seven Years Ago. Here's What Happened Next," CNN, June 9, 2020. www.cnn.com.
41. Quoted in Andrew, "This City Disbanded Its Police Department Seven Years Ago."
42. Quoted in Russell Berman, "The State Where Protests Have Already Forced Major Police Reform," *The Atlantic*, July 17, 2020. www.theatlantic.com.
43. Quoted in Berman, "The State Where Protests Have Already Forced Major Police Reform."
44. Quoted in Astead W. Herndon, "How a Pledge to Dismantle the Minneapolis Police Collapsed," *New York Times*, September 26, 2020. www.nytimes.com.
45. Quoted in Herndon, "How a Pledge to Dismantle the Minneapolis Police Collapsed."
46. Quoted in John Eligon and Kay Nolan, "When Police Don't Live in the City They Serve," *New York Times*, August 18, 2016. www.nytimes.com.
47. Quoted in Herndon, "How a Pledge to Dismantle the Minneapolis Police Collapsed."

48. Quoted in Cassandra Basler, "Connecticut State Police Union to Challenge Officer Complaint Disclosures," WSHU Radio, October 15, 2020. www.wshu.org.
49. Quoted in Kelan Lyons and Mark Pazniokas, "Police Contest the First Draft of a Police Reform Bill," CT Mirror, July 17, 2020. https://ctmirror.org.
50. Quoted in Lyons and Pazniokas, "Police Contest the First Draft of a Police Reform Bill."
51. Quoted in *Tyler (TX) Morning Telegraph*, "Houston Rep. Garnet Coleman: TCOLE Agrees to Add Implicit Bias Training to Basic Peace Officer Courses," June 8, 2020. https://tylerpaper.com.
52. Quoted in Stephanie Pagones, "Philadelphia Police Commissioner Defends Department Amid Criticism over Lack of Tasers," Fox News, October 30, 2020. www.foxnews.com.

American Civil Liberties Union (ACLU)

www.aclu.org

Founded in 1920, the ACLU focuses on pursuing legal actions on civil rights issues and most recently has been campaigning for police reform. By accessing the link for Racial Justice on the organization's website, visitors can learn about court cases the ACLU has filed against city police departments seeking justice for victims of police misconduct.

Campaign Zero

www.joincampaignzero.org

Campaign Zero works with public officials to focus on solutions and policies that lead to safer interactions between citizens and police. By accessing the link for Reports, visitors can find Campaign Zero's study of which American police departments routinely use force in making arrests.

Center for American Progress

www.americanprogress.org

This nonpartisan policy institute has taken on the issue of police reform. By accessing the link for Criminal Justice on the group's website, visitors can find the report *Assessing the State of Police Reform*, which looks at how communities are changing how their police do their jobs.

Check the Police

www.checkthepolice.org

This organization studies how labor contracts often protect police officers accused of misconduct. The group's website features a chart that shows the degrees of protection offered to police officers in sixteen states. Among those protections are rules forbidding the public from accessing police misconduct records.

Defund the Police
www.defundthepolice.org

Established by the civil rights group Black Lives Matter, this website provides information on how plans to defund the police could be implemented by communities. By accessing the link for Alternatives to Police Services, the website shows how crisis intervention specialists and other community members could step into situations formerly handled by armed police officers.

Marshall Project
www.themarshallproject.org

This nonprofit news organization focuses on stories that expose corruption in the US criminal justice system. By entering the keywords "police reform" in the website's search engine, visitors can find more than one hundred stories about efforts to reform individual police departments in America.

FOR FURTHER RESEARCH

Books

Paul Butler, *Chokehold: Policing Black Men*. New York: New Press, 2018.

Charles M. Katz and Edward R. Maguire, eds., *Transforming the Police: Thirteen Key Reforms*. Long Grove, IL: Waveland, 2020.

Alex S. Vitale, *The End of Policing*. New York: Verso, 2018.

Internet Sources

Scottie Andrew, "This City Disbanded Its Police Department Seven Years Ago. Here's What Happened Next," CNN, June 9, 2020. www.cnn.com.

Vera Bergengruen, "'We Continue to Spin in Circles.' Inside the Decades-Long Effort to Create a National Police Use-of-Force Database," *Time*, June 20, 2020. http://time.com.

Andy East, "Use of Force: Local Officers Explain How Defensive Tactics Are Taught, Monitored and Performed," *Columbus (IN) Republic*, June 13, 2020. www.therepublic.com.

John Eligon and Kay Nolan, "When Police Don't Live in the City They Serve," *New York Times*, August 18, 2016. www.nytimes.com.

Weihua Li and Humera Lodhi, "Which States Are Taking on Police Reform After George Floyd?," Marshall Project, June 18, 2020. www.themarshallproject.org.